Wealth Magick

How to attract money fast with the power of ancient magick

Table of Contents

Introduction iv

Chapter 1: Abundance through Magick 1

Chapter 2: The Basis of Magick 5

Chapter 3: Magick, Belief, and Intent 7

Chapter 5: Basic Ingredients for Spells 15

Chapter 6: Several Spells for Abundance, Prosperity, and Luck 18

Conclusion 25

Introduction

I want to thank you and congratulate you for downloading the book, *"Wealth Magick"*.

This book contains helpful information about magick and Wicca, and how it can be used to attract and create wealth!

You will soon learn about the fundamentals of magick, and discover exactly how it works. Magick can be used to attract love, romance, luck, health, and also wealth and prosperity!

This book will provide you with techniques and tips that will allow you to successfully use magick to achieve the level of wealth that you desire! It includes some simple yet powerful spells to help you achieve a life of abundance in all areas.

With the help of this guide and some dedication on your part, you'll be well on your way to creating a life of wealth and prosperity with the power of magick!

Thanks again for downloading this book, I hope you enjoy it!

Chapter 1: Abundance through Magick

How is wealth defined? Is it the sizeable amount of money in your bank account or is it a state of being or a condition, such as living a comfortable life? Does abundance entail having enough of everything or having more of everything? Such distinctions could be considered trivial, but if you seek to attain wealth through doing abundance and prosperity spells, you should be absolutely clear in your mind about what such concepts mean to you. Moreover, you also need to keep an open mind about magick (not the kind used by illusionists), and have a positive outlook in life.

Before going further, it is best to know what magick is. It is an attempt to experience, understand, and influence the world using symbols, rituals, gestures, actions, and language. A lot of contemporary Western magick practitioners generally state that magick's main purpose is personal spiritual growth.

A proper mindset is essential before embarking on unconventional ways to attract wealth. Take a few moments to define what abundance and prosperity mean to you in this moment – right now. Here, the challenge and the goal is to attain your personal prosperity through magick with intent and conscious awareness.

When casting a spell, you form your desire into a ritualized formula and motivate the full force of your emotions, will, and intentions to bring forth an outcome that is pre-determined. You then shift your energies and you feel the power in your bones, cells, and blood. Casting spells through magick brings forth a direct and immediate connection between your unconscious and conscious minds. Casting spells also awakens the inherent wisdom that has been dormant in the depths of your being.

To change your life in a positive manner means changing the way you believe and think. Prosperity spells work only if you have great faith in yourself and in the universe's capability to provide. Material bounty and money are abundant infinitely. Further to this, everyone can tap into that bounty without robbing anyone else of that abundance. If you believe you are deserving of prosperity and feel that you are valuable intrinsically, the universe will give you what you need – always. Once you have cultivated the prosperity consciousness, you can use various spells to attract abundance and riches of all kinds into your world.

Here is an example of a spell to create prosperity consciousness, which means you believe with your whole heart that you deserve to have what you want in life. You know that your good fortune does not draw away from anyone else. You also know that the universe's storehouse of goods is infinite. This prosperity spell will help you to cultivate a prosperity consciousness in order for you to do other prosperity spells successfully.

You do this prosperity spell during the new moon and the tools you need are: 14 scented green candles, one empty glass container, and an affirmation. You may ask why the candles needed are colored green. In several countries, green is the color of paper money; thus, your mind makes an automatic connection between wealth and green. However, if you happen to be living in a country where another color is prevalent on your currency, you should use that color instead to symbolize money. Silver and gold, which are precious metals' colors, are also good choices.

Prosperity Consciousness Spell

- Buy 14 green candles scented with cedar or pine essential oils. You can also use tea light and votive candles for this spell.

- During the night of a new moon, light one of the candles at your special space or at an altar, if you have one. While the candle is burning, say aloud your affirmation and feel its trueness.

- After five minutes, put out the candle and then rub your hands in the smoke. Put the smoke toward your face, clothes, and body, then waft the smoke. Recall its fragrance and liken it to prosperity, abundance, and your new belief.

- Set aside the candle. Repeat the ritual daily for the 13 remaining days, using a new candle every time. Put each spent candle beside its predecessor.

- During the night of a full moon, after the 14th candle has been burned, light all of the candles and allow them to burn down fully. Pour the leftover melted wax from the candles into the glass container; thus, forming a new candle. The new candle is a symbol of your new prosperity belief.

- Once the wax turns solid, bury it. This is a symbolic planting into the earth to make your wealth grow. It is like planting a seed, taking care of it, and waiting for the seed to sprout.

If you believe in it wholeheartedly, the prosperity consciousness spell may be enough for you. However, you may also want to understand the underlying principles that may help other spells you cast become effective in your goals to attain prosperity. Magick is not only for attracting wealth. You can also use it to attract love, peace, and harmony into your life. The following chapters will give you an overview of magick and how it makes your life, and the lives of the people around you.

Chapter 2: The Basis of Magick

Magick is all around us. Most of us will have felt magick when we were young. However, as we grow up into adults, we simply lose sight of it as day-to-day life's various stresses absorb us. Here, we want to reconnect with such magick. Here, we will also learn about nature's workings – the moon cycles and the power of the elements. You can use Nature's tools like stones, crystals, minerals, flowers, herbs, and such, in your magical workings.

Magick is especially ingrained in the principles of Wicca, which entails an individual to delve into using spells to create harmony in one's life. In a nutshell, Wicca is an age-old practice and it is an earth-oriented and gentle belief system that seeks understanding and truth. It is a way of life intended to affect inner change. It is also a framework for the use of magickal power.

While it is not necessary for modern day people to do so, Wicca involves the worship of ancient Pagan deities and observes Divine duality as a force that incorporates both the male and female – the God and Goddess. Wicca also seeks concern for the earth, encourages respect for Mother Nature, and deems that the force of life should as well be reverenced in everything.

Wicca has no rigid dogma and you can easily work Wicca and magick into your existence. Casting Wicca spells is a highly personal experience. As there is no single way to practice magick, there are also not too many rules concerning the casting of spells. However, this does not mean that there are no rules to live by. For one, casting spells means seeking the good of all (for yourself and for the people around you) and should not cause any harm.

Wicca's true magick is not about flying on broomsticks or stirring bubbling cauldrons. The magick lies in the development of your spirituality and inner potential. You have to know that deep within you, you have the power to tap into the natural world and the universe. All you need to do is recognize and direct that potential to create good in your life. The real value of spell-casting and using magick lies in connecting with nature, getting in touch with the Divine, and getting in touch with your innate potential.

Chapter 3: Magick, Belief, and Intent

When we were children, we may have imagined that the stories of Cinderella, Snow White, Alice in Wonderland, the Wizard of Oz, Peter Pan, Beauty and the Beast, and Star Wars were real. These were the stories where we found out about potions and spells, witches, and wizards, and the constant struggle between good and evil. Through fairy tales, our world was full of magick. However, like Peter Pan, we grew up and magick diminished from our lives. We do recapture some of that lost magick through movies and books like Harry Potter and Lord of the Rings, but we really do have to remind ourselves of what we have lost since we were younger.

In any spell, the core of it is your belief. Without belief, you only have gestures and words, dust and light, and nothing but bluster. It is like having Dorothy and her companions exposing the Wizard to be an ordinary man. What defines belief exactly? Let us go to Oz to seek that definition. The Lion needed courage because he believed he was a coward. Such belief ruled the lion until the Wizard told him how he really was courageous. The Lion then knew that he had courage all along. The belief in his lack of courage was what crippled him.

Going back to Wicca, are simple spells less powerful than complicated ones? The answer is that one is not better or worse than the other. The simplicity or complexity of a spell must fit the situation and the results desired. If you have a busy life and lack spare time, simple spells may be more appropriate for you than the complicated ones.

For instance, we may seek abundance. To many of us, that could be money in the bank, financial abundance, or maybe freedom from worrying about your debit or credit card being declined. For others, however, life is seemingly abundant. You may have a job that you love, great friends, and a wonderful family. There are times when a change in your beliefs occurs because another person points out that you really have what your desire. There are also times when you come to that conclusion on your own. Either way, your beliefs shift and your reality changes.

Beliefs are Powerful

A belief is accepting something as true. The world in general had believed some things as fact before other people proved them otherwise. One such case is Christopher Columbus disproving the belief that the world is flat. On a more personal note, our own personal beliefs completely surrounds us. There are some common ingrained beliefs (not always positive) that people live by including:

- My health is bad.
- Money is the source of all evil.
- I'm trapped.
- I do not live in a safe world.
- I'll never find the right significant other for me.
- I do not deserve wealth, love, or a great job.

The basis for such limiting beliefs are established during childhood when we adopt the beliefs of authority figures like teachers and parents. Our societies and cultures we live in also shape our beliefs. For example, a Western woman would not have the same beliefs as a woman in a

Muslim country. You don't need to be a victim of childhood conditioning. With intent, passion, and will, you can define for yourself what you don't believe or believe, what you don't desire or desire.

Desire and Intent

A spell's purpose is to manifest something that you desire or need. In the case of this book, that would mean prosperity and abundance. Such a desire or need (or both) comprise your intent. As you cast a spell, your intent is as significant to your beliefs as your success.

It is not difficult to define your intent as we do it all the time. On a particular day, we make choices that are evident in various ways and we do it without doing magick or casting spells. While we don't always acknowledge it, our intent creates magick in our existence constantly. Despite our delight and astonishment when magick happens, we normally consider it as coincidence and forget about it later.

Defining Wants and Desires

Defining what you want should be relatively easy. When we do it, a lot of us are aware of what we want in an instant; however, we don't have a clue when it comes to the long-term. We are absorbed in the trees yet we don't see the forest. As you attempt to figure out what you want to accomplish with your magick, be patient and honest. Take your time and know that the universe is never in a hurry.

The Role of Nature in Magick

To enhance your spell-casting, you should get in touch with the natural world. Nowadays, we consider our 'natural world' to be the world of the Internet, computers, and sealed offices. We often take for granted the actual natural world' as the wind that blows through your hair as you walk, the light of the moon, or the birds that reside in the nearby lake. The natural world can also be trees that you climbed as a child or the herb garden and the flowers that you plant.

The lunar cycles are also a part of the natural world and are important when it comes to casting spells. Each month, the moon undergoes eight various phases. For half the month, from the new to the full moon, the moon is increasing in size, or waxing. These first two weeks are a good time to cast spells that deal with expansion and manifestation. The waning phase (shrinking in size), or the second half of the month, is great for spells that deal with decrease.

Why would you want to cast decreasing spells when you need abundance in life? The decreasing spells are vital if you want to decrease debt or decrease responsibilities. Decreasing spells are cast if you wish to streamline your life, like letting go of toxic relationships or losing weight.

The new moon is also best if you want to plant symbolic seeds that detail what you want to create in your life. This is the best time to cast spells for prosperity, starting an artistic endeavor, starting a business, starting a relationship, or getting pregnant. In a particular month, there are two new moons. The Black Moon – or the second new moon – is deemed more powerful than a regular new moon. Thus, be sure to do seeding spells during the Black Moon for quicker manifestation.

Gratitude

Gratitude, in life in general as well as in magick, is one of the most valuable attributes that you must cultivate. It is crucial to accept the compliments and good things that come to you with a gracious thank you. You should know that this is the universe's way of recognizing your individuality. Gratitude in inherent in any spell; thus, you must end your prosperity spells with a gratitude expression.

Chapter 4: A Sacred Space for Magick

Many practitioners of magick would agree that one's magick place could be a temple, if one considers that it is. Sacredness is more of a matter of behavior and attitude than of trappings. It doesn't require neither props nor buildings. Having a sacred space for magic is vital, nonetheless, and there are processes and tools that Wiccans utilize to make magickally safe havens for their practice.

In magick and in Wicca, you will often perform spells in a Circle. Moreover, group spells, particularly gatherings wherein there are public rituals, normally occur in a 'sacred space' that is circular. A Circle indicates that every person present is important to the overall working's success. Also, the Circle represents accord, unity, a safe psychic sphere, and wholeness, wherein which all can find protection and comfort.

Before casting a Circle, you must have your own power spot, which is a personal space where you do your prosperity magick. There are people who have a particular spot that remains intact from casting a spell to casting the next spell. In addition, others prefer to do magick anywhere they please. One night, they may work in the garage and the next night, they may work in the yard. You should choose a spot that gives you privacy and makes you feel comfortable when performing spells.

Outside Locations

It takes intuition and time to find a power spot among natural elements. You should find a spot that feels right, even if you seek to cast your wealth magick in the backyard. This can be done by walking through your chosen outside area and be mindful of any intense or unusual body sensations: a chill, cold, heat, or even a cozy warmth in your stomach. If you are attuned to those sensations, then you will easily be able to choose the right space for you to practice your craft.

Another way to find the right spot is dowsing, which was originally used to locate water. The concept is using a tool like a forked stick to sense the location of what you seek. The stick dips down to point to the best location. You may use a forked willow branch or make a dowsing rod made from wire hangers. To make the tool work, you must infuse it with purpose and intent.

Interior Locations

When doing prosperity magick, there are people that favor interior power spots with minimal furniture. However, it depends because there are also magick practitioners who like to surround themselves with objects that remind them of enchantment and magick. Create an atmosphere that is peaceful and calm; remove anything noisy or distracting that could disturb your atmosphere.

It is helpful to do your work in an area with pastel walls and floors. If the floor is wood or tiled, get a throw pillow or rug that matches or complements the wall's color. You can also use the rug or pillow to sit on while doing magick. Aside from a pillow, you will also need a surface to put your things on. This surface can be a board put up on bricks or just even a casual wooden box. This surface can also be ornate. If you happen to favor an object (a stone, statue, or crystal), keep this object in the place where you do spell-casting. Make it a power object that will retain the magickal atmosphere, or consider it the guardian of your sacred space.

If you do not have a perfect spot to work on your prosperity spells, you don't need to worry. Just bring your passion, belief, and intent to any spell you are casting and you will be fine.

Chapter 5: Basic Ingredients for Spells

The key to great food, according to any good cook, lies in how they use and combine the ingredients. This also holds true in spells. If the ingredients are not correctly measured, and if the timing for mixing them is a bit off (or if you do not allow it to properly stew), the magick goes astray. The ingredients add 'flavor' to the magick and such has always been the case throughout magick history.

What is a good spell component? It is anything that is vital to the recipe or spell. It is anything that builds up the energy of a spell. It is also vital for the ingredients to blend well on a metaphysical level as such energy needs both congruity and continuity. Below are a few (if not all) of the basic ingredients needed to do crucial prosperity spells. You do not need to have every bit of these ingredients. All you need are a few staples that are important in the spells you cast. As you gain more experience, you will be able to create your own list of ingredients of what you need for your magick.

Aromatic Oils

The sense of smell is so strongly connected to memory that even a single scent can virtually conjure any detail and bring you back instantly to the different phases of your life. It just takes a whiff of a particular scent, of fresh-baked pies, of sea air, and even just memories. Thus, it is not surprising that love spells use aromatic oils extensively.

Just as you would a stone or crystal, you can also charge aromatic oils for spells. Just put the bottle on the windowsill where light is likely to hit it. You can request certain things from the oil or you can just say a prayer over it. Leave it on the windowsill for an hour and use it afterwards. Some of the aromatic oils used in in prosperity spell-work are bayberry, cedar, honeysuckle, mint, and patchouli. Aside from aromatic oils, you may also want to keep herbs handy. Some herbs for money magick spells are acacia, basil, chamomile, laurel, and mint.

Incense

In magick, incense has various functions. The specially prepared blends like myrrh and cedar clean the air of any undesired energies. The smoke also carries prayers and wishes to the winds. In such cases, the aroma should match the wish's intention. Moreover, the burning incense could represent either the air or the fire element in your sacred space.

Candles and Colors

Color is intrinsic to the world around us. However, a lot of us take colors for granted. Science has proved that colors hold a certain vibration or a tone that particularly touches us. Pale greens, blues, and pinks are tranquil. Red energizes and stimulates. Gold and yellow lift the spirits.

In casting spells, the colors used are important in the spell's power. Gold or green are appropriate for attracting abundance, money, and prosperity. You can incorporate certain colors in your spells when using cloths to cover your quartz crystals, candles, gems, and your altar.

In fact, candles are key ingredients in many spells. They can be used as the spell's focus or as components that set the overall tone and mood of the spell. When filled with personal power, the candles offer protection and give a way to focus attention. Lighting a candle means lighting up energy. Carving a candle means the user's intention. Pinning a candle marks a melting spot where you will release magick.

The candle's symbolic value goes further. The flame symbolizes the fire element, which signifies passion, inspiration, cleansing, and energy. You can easily use spells that need a source of fire as a component, or focus on using a candle instead of a traditional bonfire. In various rituals, candles mean the presence of the Spirit, the individual's soul, or one of the elemental powers. The colors of candles used in money magick spells include gold, green, yellow, and purple.

Now that you know the basics when it comes to casting prosperity spells, you are now ready to cast those spells in order for you to improve your life as well as your finances. It also helps to have the right mindset and the right attitude when it comes to casting prosperity spells. The next chapter contains some useful spells that you can use to bring on specific events in your life. There are spells for launching new ventures, going on a trip, or just to increase your wealth altogether.

Although these spells are provided, you can also create your own. Using the same principles explained so far, you can create your own spells by focusing your desire and intent, and creating a simple affirmation to repeat.

Chapter 6: Several Spells for Abundance, Prosperity, and Luck

Spell for Launching a New Venture

Whether you are planning to start a business, take on a new project, or even start a new job, this spell may help you in making a successful start. One of the most daunting things in life is starting a new venture and if you listen and give in to your fears, you will not know how successful you could have been. As such, it is worth noting of the significance of the color yellow, which is the color of creativity and optimism. It also corresponds to the solar plexus chakra, which is self-confidence's center. For good measure, you should perform this spell nine days before the full moon. For this spell, you will need one piece of yellow paper, 1 quartz crystal, and 1 pen (or marker or pencil).

- Have ready a word that symbolizes your goal or describes the project that you are about to undertake. After that, design a magickal sigil with the letters in the word and draw it on the yellow paper. Imagine your intention in your mind while you make the sigil and, into the drawing, project your thoughts. If you desire, you can decorate the drawing with symbols and pictures that are relevant to your venture.

- Lay the sigil face up on the altar. Set the quartz crystal on top of the sigil. On the full moon's night, burn the drawing while you are imagining yourself succeeding at your project; thus, releasing your intention into the universe. Carry the crystal in your purse, briefcase, or pocket, or set in in your workstation.

Spell for Getting a Better Job

Times are hard nowadays and you may not always land the job that you desire. In this case, use your magick skills and get busy to create the perfect job for you. This spell is best done during the waxing moon. The preferred days for doing this spell are on Thursdays or Sundays. The tools needed are: paste, glue, or tape; an orange marker; pictures from the Internet or magazines; and a piece of cardboard or paper that allows you to stand on it (if needed, tape together two or more sheets).

- Cut out the pictures that represent the different facets of your desired job. After that, cast a circle round the area where you will do your spell.

- On the cardboard or paper, use the marker to draw a symbol that is called 'the Part of Fortune', which is a design that resembles an X with a circle around it. Make your drawing big enough so that you can paste your pictures inside the symbol's quadrants. Start attaching the collected pictures to the four quadrants of the Part of Fortune symbol. While working, imagine yourself successful and happy in your new job.

- As you are done, lay the cardboard/paper on the floor. Remove your footwear and stand in the middle of the cardboard. Close your eyes and imagine becoming one with your new venture. Make your vision as real as you possibly can. Stand there until your mind begins to wander. Step off the cardboard/paper and open the circle. Until you get your dream job, repeat the magick spell as needed.

A Spell to Get Rid of Debt

You could go nuts receiving calls and demand letters from collection agencies. However, there is a magick spell that can help you say bye-bye to your debt and, in the process, those collection agencies. You need to do this spell during the waning moon. The tools needed to perform this magick are cedar wood shakes, sticks, or chips; five pentacles from a tarot deck you are not using; and one large cauldron or pot.

- Put the cedar inside the cauldron or pot, which represents fertility and creativity. Cedar also represents prosperity. Set the wood on fire. When your wood is burning, drop the tarot card into the fire. This five of pentacles card means poverty and debt. As the card burns, visualize your debts also disintegrating.

- Allow the fire to completely burn down. Collect the ashes afterward. On the night before the next new moon, bury the ashes as far away as you can take them.

Prosperity Oil

This magickal potion is highly versatile and can be used alone or together with other spells. You can dress candles with it or you can dab it on sigils or talismans. You can also anoint crystals, magick tools, or gemstones with it, or even rub a little of it on your body. Whichever way you use it, this oil helps you attract many forms of abundance.

This spell can be performed during the waxing moon, especially on a Thursday. The tools needed are: silver or gold glitter; a few drops of peppermint oil; four ounces of almond, grape seed, or olive oil; a piece of aventurine or tiger's eye stone; and a green glass bottle with a stopper or lid.

- First, wash the gemstone and bottle with water and mild soap. Dry them. Afterwards, cast a circle around the area where you will perform your magic spell.

- Pour the oil into the bottle and add the glitter and peppermint essential oil. Drop the stone into the mixture. Put the stopper or lid on the bottle and shake the bottle three times to charge your mixed potion. After that, open the circle and apply your newly-formulated Prosperity Oil in any way you choose.

Spell for Becoming a Millionaire

Having not to think about where to get money is perhaps a good thing. Who doesn't want to be a millionaire? Many people do not believe they can become millionaires and this is why they still don't have their millions of dollars. This spell reprograms your subconscious so that you can start believing that you can get millions of dollars. The most important thing here is believing that you deserve your millions.

This magick spell is to be done during the waxing moon. The tools needed are a likeness of a $1 million bill and an 'abundance' crystal or a clear quartz crystal. This stone can contain chlorite, which is a greenish mineral.

- Get a likeness of a $1 million bill, which image you can download from the Internet. You can also cut a piece of paper the shape and size of a bill. Write 'One Million Dollars' on it. If you like, your can add other images so that the bill looks as realistic as you think it can.

- Put the bill face up on your altar, desk, or in your home's wealth sector. To find the wealth sector, stand by your home's entrance, with your back to the door. The left hand rear corner is the home's wealth sector. With soap and mild water, wash the crystal. Set it up on top of the $1 million bill.

- Several times each day, pick up the bill. Stare at the bill as you recite the affirmation, "I now have $1 million free and clear, to do with as I please. This money comes to me in harmony with Divine Will, my own true will, and for the good of all, harming none. I deserve this money and I accept it thankfully." Until you succeed, keep on repeating this spell.

Spell for Recognition

Sometimes, to get ahead financially, we need to have our efforts recognized by the relevant people. Maybe your boss overlooks your hard work and does not give you credit for your contribution to the organization. Maybe customers and clients seemingly do not appreciate when you go the extra mile for them. If you feel that your efforts are not being recognized, this magick spell can help you get the recognition you feel you deserve.

Perform this spell during a waxing moon, preferably on a Thursday. The tools your need are: potting soil, 1 ceramic pot, water, and 9 seeds for a plant that blooms with purple or red flowers.

- Fill the pot with the potting soil and put the 9 seeds at different spots in the soil. As the seeds are planted, say aloud, "As I plant these seeds, I draw to me, the one who sees, what I can be. So mote it be."

- As the seeds begin sprouting, the person who recognizes your achievements should come into your life. Take care of your plant lovingly until that happens. Meanwhile, you should also try to make contacts. You never know who your 'angel' could be.

Keep-It-Coming Prosperity Circle

You may be satisfied with your current finances, but you cannot predict what the future holds when it comes to money and prosperity. This spell makes sure that – to cover your expenses - you will always have more than enough. Do this spell daily and begin during the waxing moon. The tools you need are: a pen that writes silver, gold, or green ink; a piece of paper; coins (any denomination); and nine small jars (you can use baby food jars).

- Find a spot in your workplace or home where you can permanently leave the jars in position. This should be a place where your jars will not be disturbed. Cast a circle around the place where your will perform your magick spell. In a circle, arrange the empty jars.

- On paper, write the affirmation, "I now have plenty of money for everything I need and desire and plenty to share with others." Put the paper in the center of the jar circle, and put a coin on top to secure the paper.

- Beginning at the east and in a clockwise direction, drop a coin in each jar. Every time you put a coin in a jar, repeat aloud the affirmation. Open the circle.

- The following day, add another coin to each jar. Start at the east and work clockwise. Continue this way and add one daily to each jar. When the jars are all full, take the coins out and donate the money to charity. While giving the money away, say this affirmation three times, "I offer this money with gratitude and love. I now receive my tenfold return, with good to all concerned."

- Fill the jars again in the same way as before. Keep on doing this magick spell and indefinitely share your wealth. This way, you can forever keep prosperity coming toward you.

Conclusion

Thank you again for downloading this book!

I hope this book was able to help you learn more about wealth magick!

The next step is to put this information to use, and begin creating the wealth and prosperity that you desire with the power of magick!

Finally, if you enjoyed this book, please take the time to share your thoughts and post a review on Amazon. It'd be greatly appreciated!

Thank you and good luck!

www.ingramcontent.com/pod-product-compliance
Lightning Source LLC
LaVergne TN
LVHW021748060526
838200LV00052B/3549